ULFHILDR

MARY THALER

ILLUSTRATED BY NIV SEKAR

Untimely Books

Untimely Books

untimelybooks.com
An imprint of Cosmos Cooperative
PO Box 3, Longmont, Colorado 80502
info@untimelybooks.com

Book design by Kayla Morelli
Cover art and illustrations by Niv Sekar

This is a work of fiction. Names, characters, places, and incidents either are the product of the author's imagination or are used fictitiously, and any resemblance to actual persons, living or dead, businesses, companies, events, or locales is entirely coincidental.

Publisher's Cataloging-in-Publication Data
Names: Thaler, Mary, author.
Title: Ulfhildr / Mary Thaler.
Description: Longmont, CO : Untimely Books, 2023. | Summary: On an unnamed coastline, hidden in the mists of history, a woman is confronted with her husband's death in battle, drawing on her courage and cunning to secure the safety of herself and her young son and to lead her kingdom into war. But in this brutal society, where life is cheap, she is the only person who can decide when she has gone too far.
  Ulfhildr is an epic poem in 3 parts, written (approximately) in Anglo-Saxon meter. Featuring a heroine as post-tragic as she is powerful—as daring as she is doomed—in a poetic *tour de force* told with ruthless economy, this book will prompt deep questions concerning leadership, love, and fate.
Identifiers: LCCN 2023947869 | ISBN 9781961334038 (paperback), 9781961334045 (ebook)
Subjects: LCSH: Canadian poetry -- 21st century. | LCGFT: Epic poetry. | BISAC: POETRY / Epic | POETRY / Canadian | POETRY / Women authors.
Classification: DDC 811.6s
LC record available at https://lccn.loc.gov/2023947869

CONTENTS

FOREWORD

by Marco V Morelli

J.F. Martel, in *Reclaiming Art in the Age of Artifice*, recounts the following illuminating anecdote about the nature of art:

> In 1917 the ballet impresario Sergei Diaghilev commissioned a new libretto from Jean Cocteau. When the young poet asked for advice on how to proceed, Diaghilev replied with the simple directive: "Astonish me."

Martel goes on to declare that "Art is astonishment and is born of astonishment." He elaborates: "To be astonished is to be caught unawares by the revelation of realities denied or repressed in the everyday."

I could not better describe the effect that Mary Thaler's *Ulfhildr* had on me when I first read it—and even more so when I fathomed its depths—than to say I was *astonished*.

No doubt, some part of my astonishment stemmed from the stark difference in temperament between the *person* of Mary Thaler I had come to know as a colleague—eminently even-tempered, practical, and kind—and the *artist* of the word-hoard you are invited to feast on in these pages.

Yet once I got past that initial shock, I discovered a work that spoke for itself, challenging and compelling me to step outside our everyday reality and consider a moral universe where the force of fate, embodied in the violence of men, could be powerfully confronted by the agency and equally violent determination of a woman.

Queen Ulfhildr is a post-tragic figure, whose complexity is masterfully woven in Thaler's poetic telling. Though Ulfhildr begins as a "peace-weaver," her husband's presumed death and the existential risk his absence poses to her clan requires that she reclaim her namesake as the "Wolf-Queen," navigating political intrigue, encounters with the supernatural, and even the harsh judgments of her female kin, to fight and die in accord with a code of honor she must ultimately own for herself.

There are *many* lines in this poem—combinations of wisdom-words, illustrious images, and adept alliterations—that will sear themselves into any sensitive reader's imagination. Among my favorites:

> Wolf-Queen they call you,
> Whose paws guard a son   past the age of fostering.
> The best place for him   to learn boldness and courage
> Is from a woman   who befriends no weaklings.
> But who could fear wave-depths,   when a heart-chambered ocean
> More salt-bitter and lightless   is bound in
> his veins?

Later, Ulfhildr shares the following counsel with her young son:

Seek the thoughts behind men's words,
Hidden goals in their deeds.   But your greatest rigour, save
For looking-over of self.   Find out what you want.
When you know it, be steadfast.   And never despair
Over-hastily.

Ulfhildr is a woman who may seem to belong in the mists of Nordic mythology, yet she is able speak with utter directness the most modern of truths:

There is more than one way   to manage your life.

Among its most thought-provoking themes, the poem is especially a meditation on *leadership*—not because Ulfhildr's choices are right or wrong, or she heeds the correct advice, or even that she holds the best intentions, but because in the face of overwhelming circumstances, in a male-dominated world, when she might have remained passive in her assigned role, she nonetheless acts; she *chooses to choose*; she embodies her "dark feminine" side and its terrible agency. Finally, she embraces the consequences of her choices without blame.

As the Queen goes on to declaim:

> Some build a wall   when a storm-tide rises;
> I made myself a boat,   going to meet the greater risk,
> Since the littler danger   I liked even worse.
> What weal I have got,   I wove with my weapons.

Get ready for Ulfhildr.

ULFHILDR

ULFHILDR PART ONE

In that far-distant country,   as foal-time approached,
Their granges and homesteads   began to gall our forefathers.
Their blood, like the pale,   bitter blood of the poplar,
Rose up when the ice's grip   eased on the sea-lanes.
Then kings would dream   of cattle-raids and treasure.
The young braves are bickering.   He bids them come to him.
"Search out my sword.   Drag the smith from his bothy.
On the cliff's brow set blankets   to bide in sleepless watching."
It is done. But he sends daily.   Does the ice clear yet?
Can his ship soon slide seaward   on shims of cut pine?
Or will the wealth of his kingdom   wane into nothing
And its stature sink   in the sagas of men?

Thus, warlike Thorstein,   the thanes' chosen king,
Uttered a feast-day,   an end to Lent's fasting.
Brightly the ale flowed.   Soon blood would flow likewise.
Though he strewed rings among them,   he bestowed yet more daggers.
Men clamoured to declare   their courage loudest,
Wasting their voices   over the wild tumult,
When beside their lord   she silently appeared.

The cup, which the Queen   carried to each man,
Neither partial nor devious,   but in perfect justice,
Brimmed with mead,   to bless and speed sea-ward.
Each cinched his sword-belt   and swore his great oath
Not to waver, and still more   never to flee.
They abandoned their benches   at break of day,
But it takes such a host   a long time to pass by.
The shadows would fall   on the sheep-folds and byres,
Covering the empty cots,   and the cattle still plainting
Before their feet's echo   had faded from the shingle
And she hung the heavy bar   on the hall's massive door.

What rout has been here?   What riot of trenchers?
Whose bitter hatred   heaped on these mead cups?
Above them she strode   like a bright shield-maiden,
But in deeds a good spirit,   dressing each thing to rights.
She startled when a voice   spoke from the shadows,
    "Fair Lady," it said,   "White Lamp of your people,
Who mirrors day's light   when murky distance drowns it,
Long life and Victory!"

                    Little liked the Queen
This overbold greeting.   Her eyebrows lowered,
She spoke thus   to the concealed intruder,

"For five hours blue furrows   have flowed under my lord's keel,
Turning clods of white foam.   Battle's clamour awaits him.
It awaits all noblemen,   all wishing for nobility,
All hearts stirred by glory.   Who, then, would linger?
Do you fear murky depths,   the vast fosse of monsters
Above which the tempest   barely mars the sea-skin?
Or coldness in battle,   when a comrade stands reeling,
Lost to common sense,   until his limbs are hacked off?
Or do meaner purposes   than mere cowardice
Turn away your thoughts   from war-won renown?
Speak hastily! For this household   hates both thieves and cravens."

"Well said, Ulfhildr.   Wolf-Queen they call you,
Whose paws guard a son   past the age of fostering.
The best place for him   to learn boldness and courage
Is from a woman   who befriends no weaklings.
But who could fear wave-depths,   when a heart-chambered ocean
More salt-bitter and lightless   is bound in his veins?
Or be spooked by battle,   seeing that to avoid it,
Promises no defence   from piercing blades?
The truth is, war's glory   taunts my spirit
As far beyond me   as mighty feats to a child.
No matter his mettle,   a man cannot do combat
When withheld, as I am,   from the help of a sword."

The Queen's pride turned to pity,   and she replied quickly:
"Men guess, but can't know,   what grief may await them.
Wounds won in battle,   or weariness, the badge
Of that cunning opponent,   cold-fingered time,
Befit men as fairly   as forged armour or swords."

He laughed. "Unlicensed blood,   not large-famed feats,
Have coloured my tale.   Kin-strife, which the villain
Dares not avow: the death of a brother."

Seeing her kindness   so sadly misplaced,
The Queen replied: "No crime of men
Spatters with sin   like the slaughter of family.
What kind of victory   can they expect?
Sorrow, not swords,   is what our souls' Guardian gives
To a kin-slayer's hand."

                    From the corners of the hall
No answer came back.   She asked if she had heard
The bodiless words   of a banished ghost.
Before the Queen   finished with her tasks,
She laid an old rug   lengthwise over the sill.
A distant breeze   lapped the door of the hall,
Colder than the sea,   and cunning of entry.

Where the first waves   wash the grey beach
Shield-lights are flickering,   shouts echoing.
Billows of blood   disturb bream and herring.
Thorstein calls to his thanes   as he thrusts with his sword
Bodies of slain,   brother and foe together,
Before their feet, while,   firm behind their shoulders,
The ships, their final refuge.   A shoaling tide
Will save or erase   these stubborn fighters.

In her husband's hall,   Ulfhildr awoke,
Ears filled with battle-cries,   eyes with dark visions.
If the reed-thatched roof,   the rafters above her
Broke over her head,   they could be no heavier.
Her soul weak within her,   she sought the open vault
Of the towering sky,   the tale-bearing wind-road.

"If my heart hears riders   at the hintermark, circling,
Then palisade and bank   must be pulled down already.
I know that the man   who never fled a fight,
He whose smile was my sunlight,   the sword-thanes' captain,
My lord and friend,   now lies below-ground.
A wife recognizes   these whispered auguries.
Striving for his soul,   the sea and land,
Have offered, like envoys,   iron, gold,

And lying promises.   Now the living are bereft.
What can men count on?   Sinews weaken. Only kinship
Can hold up your arm   when heaven strikes.
But what of those facing   the world too soon,
Who have neither gold,   nor any family?
My son, your father   sleeps below the earth.
Will they let you keep your life   when they have looted your honours?"

Mind-breaking grief,   the wise mother unburdened,
Nor awaited comfort.   But at once from the shadows
She heard the Kin-slayer: "This heart-deep out-pouring
Is seemly for a widow,   but strange from a shield-maiden
Who laid hand upon helm   in the hall of her father,
And swore, while she lived,   never to see her fame dim,
Nor leave alive   any foe whom she feared."

"It's true in my youth   I often took up the spear,
And a man would think twice   before meeting me in battle
Had he heard of my deeds.   But though my hand knew warlike tools,
I long since set them down   and learned peace-weaving,
Disdaining to act   as did the old queens,
And let my lust for power   lead me to meddle
Or stir up trouble.   By some uncanny means
You have gained this knowledge,   forgotten by nearly everyone."

The Kin-slayer replied, "In calmer years
Skills of peace-making   were sought and prized.
In times past, men guarded   their own torp and byre,
Nor brooked that a proud ruler   should bend their necks.
It was rumours of marauding bands,   ruffians, and other dangers,
That herded house-men   to the high moot-place.
They demanded some brave man   mount the seat,
Owned lordship to the one   who could lead them forth.
Fear conquers pride.   It forms the kingdom's warp
Upon which is woven   the weft of fame.
Now, when the enemy   is northward massing,
A shield-maiden should rise,   and with loud shouts warn
Her people, speak of both   their peril and her Queenship."

Ulfhildr heard,   and, heeding, tarried not
To wake her husband's thanes — those ones that remained.
They came yawning and stood   in the yard, weapons loose,
She spoke. "Now I see   how uncertain I should feel
When I realize where I am,   surrounded, not by warriors
But bewildered children   awake past bed-time.
Do you spy the smoke   streaming from the North?
Or can you see   the crows line the beach?
Intelligence rides the wind;   they talk and plan
A journey that ends   in a juicy feast.

Must I tell you   that your master is fallen?
Or hasn't the upheaval   in your hearts forewarned you?
We who have enjoyed   what our lord won for us of riches
Can feel no safety,   when our defender has perished.
I will strike our foes,   my strength blot them out,
So the place on the hilltop   which they prepared for attack
Will be scoured, as the waves   sweep the bare rocks.
Thus in Paradise,   Thorstein will be glad
While we will know, in us,   no weakness can be found."

Hrothar, who had raided   with the reindeer-herders in his youth,
Next plundering southward,   a passage through vineyards,
By hardihood winning   highest praise, and a feared name,
At the speech of the Queen,   swung down his shield.
"If I guard for the future   just one grain of my strength,
Left uncast in this broil,   you may call as worthless
The feats of my arms.   This firm-minded woman
Gives us lessons in boldness.   She will lead me, and gladly."

But Haki, whose broken knee,   unhealed by rune-branches,
Made the warriors think   he could work more good at home
Improving, with new ploughs   or other plans, their oat acres,
Also stood in that yard.   He spoke without fear.
"What a long list of men,   after losing a dear one,

Have shuddered as loneliness   shut, wave-cold
Overhead. Now they see   their best helper has left them.
Whatever floats, they grasp at.   I felt this way once.
Now I can tell you: you must know the difference
Between your right wits   and the tumbling flood!
If your sword-arm is sound,   you can decide what is right.
Shall we go forth in haste,   giving up all strategy,
Onto unknown ground?"

                    This truculent speech
Gave Ulfhildr check.   But the others reckoned Haki
Of a lawless kenning.   While his leg's stubborn wound
Would not bend to the healer,   it was better not to look into
His fey, hidden mind.   Fourteen swords in all
Were committed that morning.   Men were there who,
Grey-haired, had served   Gorm, the father of kings.
Another, sister to Ulfhildr   by solemn marriage,
Named Valka, a spear-wielder   and victor of foot-races.
There were others, more fierce   than their ages could give proof.
With Haki, and Hrothar,   and a half-dozen more,
They readied for the depth-crossing   road, their long journey.

How wise is the sight   that sees well that path
Over rough waves,   the rocks hidden
Under furrow and crest!   What you feel most sure of
Changes at the worst instant,   the choppy swell
Has traps for sailors,   and the turn of its stones
Grinds forth forever   grief and bitterness.

ULFHILDR PART TWO

At the bottom of the sound,   on a bare island, over-shadowed
By spruce-thronged shores,   there stood a hut.
A husband and wife   held it in tenure
By far-gone rite.   They were fishing people,
But their eyes had watched   for other things than fish
On this waterway.   Now they watched a king's son.
The Queen must tend this care.   She could, once all is safe,
Fly unweighted to her foes   and, unworried, enjoy,
For the loss of her beloved   lord, revenge
—but first, she says:

                    "Before you had the years
To search after wisdom,   I'd spoken to you already
Counsels I must now   put with courage to proof.
The leader is shrewdest   who looks the deepest.
Birds believe a rampart   is built for their nest-place;
Mice think a corn-rick   was meant to be their hoard.
Things have many purposes.

Seek the thoughts behind men's words,
Hidden goals in their deeds.   But your greatest rigour, save
For looking-over of self.   Find out what you want.
When you know it, be steadfast.   And never despair
Over-hastily."

So, speaking   from her heart's hoard, the Queen
Sought what wealth she could give   to her weanling; he whom fate
Did not mean her to see again.   And much of value
A listener could have learned.

Over muddy reaches,   a murk of smoke
Covers the waterways   where cries echoed
Pain and fear.   Here planked houses stood;
But what was timber   is warped and blackened.
  Chosen place, supplying   a portion of sea-riches
To its housemen—where they built   halls, and counsel places,
Winning renown   for wisdom. Their home,
Has been made at last,   a murderous pit
By sword-quenching slaughter.   The sedge-decked river
Is crammed with limbs,   cold and blood-slimed.
Drowning was the death   ordained. Never again
Will these roofs, fire-blackened,   keep the rain from their walls.

The wave-courser had worked   long and well. It rested,
Hove up, surrounded   by high sand-dunes.
Speedily it had borne   the spear-carriers to the fight.
Later its wood   chanted lays and victory-songs,
North-flying, to the wind.   There was nothing more fleet
On the many-hued waters.   So men showed it respect,
As one worthy of its guard.   But those watchers never saw
The Queen, as she climbed   through the cliffs' dark maze,
Farther into the haunts   of fateful shadow.
Who would hear   what her heart had to say
—if not the one she came   by night-cover to seek?

"Gladness must flow   in gift-giving," she said,
"I can reward my followers,   show my worth to them
With heavy gold.   My husband's kinswoman
Received rings from me   for her spear's bright deeds.
Sure-hearted in danger,   she was friend-bolstered.
No bridle of age   could bid her companions mild
When renown was on their minds.   Nothing, no fray
Less ruthless than this   could have rooted my leadership
So strongly in their breasts.   Still, worries plague me.
I was told, long ago,   this town we put to flame
Was bound to us by thick ties.   Whereby, though our foes
Had told them, through messengers,   of treasures to be won,

And made them broad pledges, they remembered their friendship
With Thorstein's hall, sealed thoroughly by gifts
And by the ties of blood. Now I fear
Today's work, though our pride never wanted to hide it,
May conceal a grim crime, of soul-maiming portent."

The headland stayed silent toward the helm-bearing Queen.
Nor could wind-stunted trees tell the woman what to do.
"This too hurts my heart's quiet: that Haki Broke-Knee,
Forbidding his wound to hold him back from feats,
Held shoulder with us for his share of fame.
He stood last winter in our sword-giver's hall,
Grimed by the salt of the grinding sea-mill,
Desiring the happiness of service to a lord
—he that for a long time, had been firmed up only
By the painful duty to repay his father's death.
The word is, that his knee, in witness of that task,
Is for now constrained never to heal
Till he carries it out. His cunning is peerless,
And his plans always the best to perplex our enemies,
But they cross my aim, that my captains' fealty
Be strengthened toward my shield. I slight him. He knows
That I troubled very little to tie him to me with gifts.

Thus I'm left guessing   at the thoughts of a man
Well-versed in hiding.   Very cheerfully
I'd go to the ocean floor,   to grapple with monsters
In darkness, or unaided   face dense spear-thickets,
Were I certain such a trial   could make me safe from his mind."

Brought by cruel worries   to the brink of oath-making,
The War-Queen finally heard   the awaited voice,
The same one that had hailed her   two days since, in her hall.
It unlocked these thoughts,   that had long been in her heart:

"You have seen how fleeting   Earth's seasons are:
Wealth scatters,   weapons rust,
And house-timbers, or the fields   which toilsome labour
Make gold in summertime,   or your gladness that friends
Surround you—none of these   can be reckoned everlasting.
We know one thing: no man, having gone
Into the earth,   ever returns.
There is small good done,   striving below that vault.
Take hold of this surety.   Let it help you to a road,
Throw light on the safe path.
                              Look: here is a knife.
One night, while rime   formed noiseless on the stones,
And the wolf herself,   in silence, seemed cowed

By the footsteps of something   more frightening than she,
I cut with this edge   my close-linked fetters.
Being freed by my iron-hearted   friend from dread,
I piled praise upon him.   But his peerless loyalty,
Though staunch, does not keep him   from serving another.
You may charge him with the task   a more cherished blade,
Being nobler in spirit,   may nicely refuse.
I don't push you toward anything   past what I believe
Can be encompassed   by a queen's hardy will."
When Ulfhildr at last   went hence from that place,
Making the track down,   her mind was fixed
On this brambling riddle: the best way that she,
Through cunning, could honourably   kill him who was
A nuisance to her.   Never did she intend
To fold her deed in shadow,   but before her war-band
Would strike.

Daybreak saw   the spear-wielders feasting
Their noble victory.   The new-minded Queen
Poured fresh no paltry   portion of mead.
Haki was with the others.   To him she raised,
With well-chosen words,   the weal-cup. "Into years
Long hence, this thane   should be lauded, and given

Full guerdon. He sweeps   the ground clear of foes,
—sweeps souls from their bodies!   See, my thanes,
Had I cleverness to skald it,   I'd conclude Haki studied
The brash ambuscades   of my broom-wielding women
When my husband took him in!"

                    Haki understands
Her speech, and replies,   "I see this lovely Queen
Growing boisterous-hearted.   After battle, it's known
That fighters, who allowed   no foe to check them,
Should behold as little need   to hem up their mirth
With surly foresight—though wise silence has kept
Many kingdoms intact.   Noble Queen, since I share
That lack of verse-gift   to lustre my words,
I must find another answer."

                "I fully believe
That you rate high at answering.   So this riddle should please you:
After taking the tallest   tree-trunk, the ship-builders
Saw an unlopped branch;   yet they stepped their mast easily.

After burning the largest   beam, the hall-raiders
Passed under the lintel;   though gore-painted, it stood unharmed.
After cutting the twig   from the crab-apple, the lover

Slipped. His axe bit root.   Now he stumbles to his wooing.
Honoured thane, say   what this is, and I'll know
In what frame you answered   your father's life-thief!"

Around them, not one person,   from Hrothar on down,
Missed the Queen's meaning,   or imagined that Haki
Could force himself   to face it meekly.
Like a warrior surrounded   by wolves, he had no choice.
    "I know what you are,   or if not, what you will be:
The queen of a gull-haunted   coast, of salt
And needles of ice,   but never of men,
Whom you led to cold graves.   Little do I expect
My words to bear weight,   when in this company
I can't vaunt myself   for a vengeance that's still unfinished.
The carrion-fiend   who clipped my family's stalk
By stabbing his brother   has stealthy powers
To travel unseen,   or tender his counsels
Across waves—to speak eerily   where he is not.
Bringing him to bay   has been far from easy.
Though the meshes of his thought   are malignly woven,
I have patience stored up   to pick out that thread
That, snapped, will leave me,   scathelessly avenged.
My mind is decided   to mete just such vengeance
—not choosing to tear   into cheerless tatters

A fabric of high value,   the friendship of peoples,
Or to gash the bond   between gift-giver and thane
With boastful riddles.   You bid me merrily
Say what this is?   Then beware what I see:
A scrimping trollwife,   who scuttles to carve,
Cutlets of oozing   corpse-flesh for her spawn."

Valka, whose anger   vied in speed with her feet
Sprang up to answer   for her slandered kinswoman,
But the She-Wolf never meant   to share the fight
She had laboured to get.   Longer speech was unneeded.
Against shrewd blows,   her shield would serve best.
Now Haki for each stroke   of hers gave back two.
Her sword, which had served her   since her youth
Was shattered in pieces.   Her shoulder hung
As if made useless.   Haki, eager to finish
This noisy broil,   grappled near to strike.
Then her seeming-hurt arm   stabbed from close-to
With the Kin-slayer's knife.   That cut short the fight.

Haki was dying.   He couldn't help but break
His vow at last,   leaving his vengeance unfinished.
With cold fingers, he felt   the flood-doors of his life

Wet and red.   "Once, I saw
What looked like this dagger.   Now it laps my blood,
But then it was my father,   the old thane, who held it.
It never came to his sons.   This clever shield-mauler
Has proven more loyal   to your part, than the master
whose life it took."

It was like a snare
That was visible only   once avoiding it was hopeless.
Now Ulfhildr understood   how, on the cliff,
She'd let herself not ask   or look deeply into
The crimes she had known   her counsellor guilty of.
Thus the man had achieved   the removal, at her hand,
Of his greatest danger.
So the gulf that yawns
Between waves may show   some poor wight how vast
The swells are that drown him.   No strand appears,
To give helpful direction.   Ulfhildr had before her
A very cold road.

ULFHILDR PART THREE

There is an hour   that, ending the day's span,
Resurfaces the tide-flats,   their silver radiance
Gloriously changing   to golden foil.
The Queen, who is far   from her country, stands
At the rail, sun-dazzled.   She recognizes the lines
And shapes that mark out   this shore. "Here, Valka
Is where I was sent   when of fosterable age.
These hills, green-shadowed,   were my hunting-ground, I
And my sword-brothers. Fearless,   we speared wild boar,
And boasted of things   we planned bravely to do.
My foster-brothers, if they live,   are famous for courage,
But arrogant. I could never   get renown while I lived
In that house. If I go   to their hall, it must be
As a queen, a war-leader   clad in my victories,
Or as nothing.

             From here,   it is nearly a day
Walking over rough ground   to our enemy; to where
They gloatingly count   their gore-spattered loot.
But this breeze, I think,   will bring us to their camp

When the moon is setting.   A good moment for those
Whose hearts are caulked   against horror's night-seeping.
    What Thorstein tried   three days since, we shall do.
Our kingdom will have   the crowning shield-hedge
Of a war-like name."
                                There was one fewer spear
To count in that host,   since the Queen led them forth.
As the sky's gold sank   in the seething waves,
She would have welcomed   some words of help.
Even the heckling   of that evil-minded spirit
Who had set her on this road   would have sounded friend-like.
She was here to contend   with her heart's inmost depth,
What to do. And the place   was one of great quiet.

The turf streams down   a torrent of cinders.
Though night has turned   another quarter,
The smaller dark   inside seems endless
To the hard-set thanes.   They hoped, when they came,
To burn down these walls,   not be the ones trapped
With their victims' bodies — a reverse that wields
A cruel edge. The slaughter,   which had ebbed their way
Flowed in deadly force   following Hrothar's death.
A good man, he gave up   that last grain, and went
From cribbed trap to an even   closer-walled grave.

Morning still drowsed   when the maiden ran up
To the buildings. Her blows   set the battens all shaking.
She had flown over sharp-cobbled   fells, through drenching
Ice-torrents, not one whit   terrorized in the dark
By the haunts of dead footpads,   hanged there for foul deeds,
Or by wolves' slinking paws.   On wings that out-paced
The raven, Valka ran,   the best race of her life.

"Throw off sleep! Your hearth-sister   stands beset, her shield
Hacked in two pieces,   hammered by sword-blows.
Seconds leap, every one   like her last from the spool.
Now is the time   to knit binding threads,
Reinforce the fetters   of affection-made boasts,
And with speed go to help.   A swordsman alone
Can't defend himself. It needs   four or five to make a wall.
Rise briskly — for Death stoops   like a brindled eagle
Over its chosen morsel!"

                    Valka's outcry rousted
Her Queen's foster-brothers,   recalling what they owed
Their embattled kinswoman.   A band of warriors
Then set on the march.   The sun had over-shot
Its noon-height when the enemy   hove into view.

Their thanes, unsuspecting,   were then at counsel.
A morning's cruel labour   the mail-clad Queen,
Had inflicted on them.   From fear of her weapons,
They dared not come close enough   to drive her out with flames.
Her foes were still debating,   when affray very suddenly
Burst upon them.   Striking blows on all sides,
Valka's sword-wielders set to work.   A swarm of javelins
Vaulted overhead.   Then Valka, who had run
The whole length of the night,   was like one just rising,
Fresh of heart, from her sleep.   She handled her sword
With fatal purpose.   Their foes were like wind-chaff.
When the rescue party arrived,   the rest soon perished.

The battle-maiden helped   her brother's wife
Under the wider sky.   The war-minded lady
Had such grievous wounds,   that the ground beneath her
Was sodden with blood.   Though she saw that the victory
In which she put hope   had been won by another,
She held back from rebuking   the heartbroken young woman,
But questioned her whether,   among the corpse-stripped loot
Any thing had been found   that was Thorstein her lord's,
Whose vengeance had brought her   this vast distance — some ring
Or other token.   None of aught had been found.

It was hard for Valka   to see Ulfhildr dying.
Salt-tears fell like hailstones.   The strength she could get
Was all in anger.   She asked, "By what road
Did we come to this waste?   I cannot imagine
How the mother of a prince,   whose matchless conduct
Was esteemed everywhere,   for strength as for wisdom,
Let her well-thought blow   fall so widely astray
That it hewed her own people.   It has the appearance
Of some baleful spirit   borrowing her will.
Now where is the meed   won in victory? And how
Do they fare, those ships   with their friend-making treasures?
The ambit of the ice-cold   ocean has swallowed them.
If, my Queen, you'd resisted   that counsellor when he
Was telling you the way   to tear up your kind hawsers,
Our hall-years would have been   much happier and longer,
Lingering near your seat   to delight in your praise."

Then Ulfhildr was angry,   as she hadn't been before.
And sternly — though with effort — she said, "Now this wrong
Passes all other injuries: that you put it about
I was weak-willed, like a ship   unwatched by its crew
Being apt to drift   onto any shore.
Wasn't I your queen?   Then what was my task
But to hear the arguments   my housemen brought me,

By word-sifting, find out   how to wend past dangers
To a path? My mind   was the pivot between
Their fraught gut-yearnings   and my effective power.
So the hinge of a brooch,   though hidden by gold weave,
Unseen, shows most plainly   the skill of its maker
Should hinge fail, the brooch goes   in a heap with other trash,
And we bid him make one new.

                    Is it bandied among men
That Ulfhildr was ill-counselled?   Let them hear this, then:
Although I have heard   that after my death
I'll be forced to recount   how fared my deeds
— Hrothar's ruined hopes,   the deadly wrangle my fear
Made me force upon Haki,   and far worse again,
The squandering of my kingdom — you can be certain that I
Will not loosen my fingers   from the least of these sins,
Though Hell lay in the balance.   No hoard-thief was ever
Driven off so jealously   than a so-deemed advisor
Sharing blame from my store.   To boldly claim my deeds
Is no less needful   to the nobleness I bear
Than a precious circlet,   or patterned sword."

Valka asked, "Was it noble   to urge fruitless slaughter,
And waste your thanes' trust?"   The wounded Queen answered:

"As I am a woman,   from my earliest days
I found opposition   from friends as much as enemies.
Men believed I would never   outlast battle's trial,
Whatever proofs I showed them.   Surprise cuts me deep
When a female voice joins   in that fatuous racket!
Now, bitter-tongued sister,   try to be more skeptical.
We have said to ourselves   it is seemlier for a woman
To hand out rich gifts   on behalf of her lord,
Or to marry off her children,   or with mead-cup in hand
Foretell men's happiness,   or walk the tilth, pouring
Milk, honey, and flour   to make the furrows green.
How pleasant Earth should be,   from her peace-weaving labour!
And how little it takes   to bring this labour to nothing.
A man's death will do it,   or a misspoken jest
Pleasantries blundering   where pride already rankles.
Then this loom-woven safety   will be like spider-down.
    On blustery nights,   fast abed in our halls
We rejoice that outside   the jarring waves,
And cruel rocks may yet keep   the raiding-parties distant.
We know if we fall   unarmed into their hands
We will be no less loot   than the boar-helms or rings
That they take from the slain.   There's no telling what will happen
To the children we bore   and cherished. And these thoughts
Work in us, until we feel   how wide the darkness is

Under the moulded gables.   We could measure it with our hands,
Feel our way to the bottom   without finding another soul.
Then crimes stop mattering — even kin-slaying seemed nothing
To me, when other people's   mere existence was doubtful.
My gaff was ready-trimmed   for the gale that would drive
So many to their deaths,   men and women both.

    Fate is strong. I had to choose   not to fret beside my loom,
Or bide, as Haki did,   for the best-chosen moment
— a scheme that served him   a sorry trick at last!
There is more than one way   to manage your life.
Some build a wall   when a storm-tide rises;
I made myself a boat,   going to meet the greater risk,
Since the littler danger   I liked even worse.
What weal I have got,   I wove with my weapons."

    Her soul was leaving her.   Now she said, "When I thought
Of the likelihood of my death,   what I longed for most
Was to see you, holding   my sword in the place
Of a daughter. But this doubt,   that I dower you only
With a stubborn grief,   gives me second thoughts.
My gear should lie buried   in my grave. When the role
That you played here has lost   its painful sting,
Then you'll have happiness,   which I think you deserve."
This was how Ulfhildr,   that high-mettled woman,
Unknotted life's bindings.   She would never find a route

Up that wandering track   of water where her son
Watched over the ebb-way.   Soon after, trained men,
Singers and royal skalds,   who had studied the way
To fashion into words   the feats of brave warriors,
Began to tell of this widow,   an intrepid ship-raider,
And dealer of wounds.   The details were well-known
Of her nerve and cunning.   But they could never agree
Whose was the voice   that had hailed her from the shadows
When alone with her thoughts.   The listeners were left wondering.
   This version was told me   by Valka the Grief-struck
In the ice-eaved hall   of the Exiled King.
That was a long way from here.

                              Thus we try each morning
To lift our spirits   with the belief we can read
The humour of the waves,   harrying those elders
Who know something about winds,   to soothsay our journey.
One man says, "I will have riches."   A second, "This gull-track
Will show its secret currents   and shores to me alone."
A third, "In half a year,   I'll be home. Someone is there
Who loves me."
          So we set out.   Laden with cargoes
Small or big.   Our sails can't always
Help where they go.   But we set out.

WRITING ULFHILDR IN
ANGLO-SAXON(ISH) METER

When writing Ulfhildr, I had in mind more historical fantasy than historical fact. The research I did was scattershot, and driven more by a futile hope of avoiding embarrassing anachronism than a sincere effort to anchor my story to real geographies and cultures. But the one historical detail I worked hardest at was inherent in the structure of the poem. I wanted to tell the story in Anglo-Saxon meter.

Meter is the rhythmic structure of lines, or what you might call the beat. In modern free verse, this patterning is up to the poet, while formal poetry is guided by stricter conventions. While a lot of the formal poetry we're familiar with also uses rhyming, you may be aware that Old English poetry, written in the seventh to eleventh centuries, used alliteration instead. The exact rules vary (and like all rules, they are meant to be broken), but for my poem, I set myself a few guidelines. The result should be construed less as historically authentic Old English meter, than as my own particular, historically tinged, flavour. Here's a short passage:

Thus, warlike **Thor**stein, || the **thanes'** chosen **king**,
Uttered a **feast**-day, || an **end** to Lent's **fast**ing.
Brightly the **ale** flowed. || Soon **blood** would flow like**wise**.
Though he **strewed** rings a**mong** them, ||

he be**stowed** yet more **dagg**ers.

First, notice that each line falls cleanly into two sections. I've marked
this break, whose technical name is a caesura, with a double vertical line.
If you're reading aloud, you can take a deep breath here (or heck, stand up
and stretch your legs) before you go on to the next half of the line.
The second thing to notice is that each half-line has two stressed syllables,
which I've marked by bolding. If you're reading aloud, feel free to thump
hard on these. This is where the alliteration comes in. Within a line, the first
and third stressed syllables must use the same sound. Sometimes the second
stressed syllable will match (as it does in the first line), but not necessarily.
The fourth stressed syllable must never match. What I love about it is that
it makes the end of the line feel strange and unsettled; thus propelling the
reader into the next line in search of resolution.

The third guideline is less a rule than a guiding value: in arranging
these lines together, I place a high value on variety. For example, no two
adjacent lines should use the same alliterative sound, and as far as possible
they shouldn't have the same rhythm either. Some sentences are complex,
like the first one in this passage, flowing from one line to the next (this is
called enjambment), while the last two lines in this passage each end with a

short, declarative sentence. You'll also notice that the first three lines of this passage start with a heavily stressed syllable, so with the fourth line I try to break up this pattern, to keep the meter from falling into a static pattern. Again, this is the antithesis of, say, iambic pentameter, the traditional meter for sonnets, which has a highly regular, almost metronome-like beat:

My **mis**tress's **eyes** are **no**thing **like** the **sun**
Coral is **far** more **red** than **her** lips' **reds**

I've written elsewhere about why I love writing formal poetry. I love it for its own beauty, and also for the skills it teaches me that apply to my other writing. It was while I was writing Ulfhildr, searching relentlessly for the right words to fit into my alliterative scheme, that I started the habit of having a thesaurus tab always open on my browser and, if I'm writing by hand, jotting lists of near-synonyms in the margin. I do this now as I revise yet another draft of my novel. I've learned that I don't have to settle for a word that is only almost good enough.

Why is it that I think the form of this poem mattered even more than details of plot and setting? Truth in storytelling is often more a matter of feeling than fact. I guess my hope for this story is that, even if Ulfhildr wasn't an authentic historical queen, the rhythm of its heartbeat will still be something real and fierce.

ABOUT THE AUTHOR

Mary Thaler is a writer, zine-maker and environmental microbiologist. She is currently revising the manuscript of a historical novel about the Arctic. Her work has appeared in numerous literary journals, and can be found online at marythaler.wordpress.com

ABOUT THE ILLUSTRATOR

Niv Sekar is an artist and writer. She grew up in the South and now resides in New York, watching the winters grow warmer. Her work is occupied with movement and time, queerness, boundaries, and the speculative. Niv can often be found working on stories about queer brown girls. Find her work here: nivsekar.com.

ABOUT UNTIMELY BOOKS

Untimely Books is an independent publisher of literary works that illumine the mind, question the contemporary, and reimagine horizons of thought, feeling, and action for a planetary age. As an imprint of **Cosmos Cooperative** (a member-owned publishing platform and creative community) and **Metapsychosis** (a journal of consciousness, literature, and art), Untimely Books serves as a conduit for diverse forms of writing by Cosmos members, including original works of fiction, poetry, philosophy, essays, and memoir.

untimelybooks.com